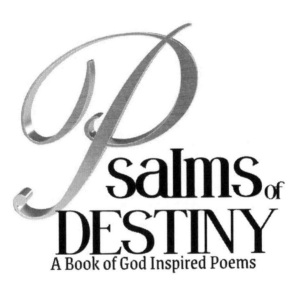

Psalms of DESTINY

A Book of God Inspired Poems

Minister
JESSICA WANSLEY

COOLBIRD
PUBLISHING
HOUSE™

Acknowledgements

I want to begin by expressing my gratitude to God for blessing me with the talent to write poetry. Initially, I struggled to appreciate my gift because I wanted to sing, but He guided me towards writing instead. Next, I would like to thank my mother, Barbara Jean Thomas, for entering me into a poetry contest at the tender age of six, which led to me receiving an honorable mention. I am also grateful to my spiritual mother, Apostle Patricia Powell, for recognizing my gift and encouraging me to embrace it. A heartfelt thanks goes to Minister Kelis McGhee of W.A.C. Ministries, my supportive husband Bryan Wansley, who often stays up with me until 2 a.m. when inspiration strikes, and my big brother Lorenza, who humorously mimics my words before attempting to read them back to me as if I don't know what I've written. Lastly, I extend my appreciation to all my friends and loved ones for their unwavering support.

About the Author

Jessica Wansley was born August 29, 1978, in Cleveland Ohio. She is the youngest of four children and the mother of three children. God called her middle child home May 2, 2014. She's a Minister at Miracle Deliverance Temple of the New Millennium Ministries located in Anniston, AL.

Currently, she resides in Gadsden, AL. While she is not sure of the age she began writing, she remembers being in elementary school and her mother entering her into a poetry contest from an ad she found in a magazine. At only 6 years old, Jessica Wansley won honorable mention. Jessica says she'd like to think that she came out of her mother's womb with a pen and piece of paper. She is a saleswoman and business owner with a small shop located in Eastaboga, AL. Jessica attests that she has experienced many tragedies and trials in this lifetime and pray her poetry will encourage and inspire someone else to go on another day.

Contents

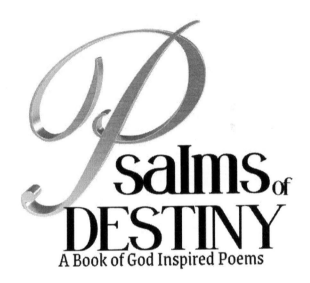

Psalms of DESTINY

A Book of God Inspired Poems

Minister JESSICA WANSLEY

God's Promises

Sunny days aren't always promised from the Lord,
He never said things wouldn't get hard,
Yet, there's sunshine beyond the rain,
And there's laughter beyond pain.
We may not understand situations we see,
However, God's presence can fill this place.
He promised to always be there,
He promised He would always care.
Seek shelter under His shadow,
Then, your strength will be renewed,
Unlike men you'll never be used,
He told us to never fear man,
For boldness and guidance,
He will always hold our hands.
He promised His everlasting love,
This is a promise from above.

Let Love

Lord, please let our love be trained and unchanged,
Let's learn the meaning of longsuffering through eternity,
Forever together let us pray,
Help us bond and never walk away,
May our love be strong steel with our marriage
  within your will,
Let us gradually grow through the years,
Committed, let us always stand,
We humbly place this marriage in your hands.

The Invitation
(Luke 7:36)

We're invited to the best celebration,
Resisting satan we've fought temptation,
It's accepted with trembling and fear,
The door isn't locked we don't have to hear.
You're not welcomed here!
The sea holds our former sins,
Invitation in hand we'll call you friend.
A second life is a great inspiration.
Gracefully, we accept this invitation.
Humbly, your saints enter your heavenly nation.

Daughter
(Mark 10:13-16)

Born in a dark light that began to shine,
I'm blessed to know God made you mine.
Much would transpire that I didn't know,
God gave a lesson on motherhood watching you grow;
Watching I had to cry seeing life pass by,
Then God told me to calm down and stop stressing,
You're more than my daughter,
You're a blessing.

Holiness or Hell
(1 Tim 2:9-10) (Genesis 2:18)

Don't try to judge by what you see,
She adds pride and courage to ministry,
Truly, a pastor after God's own heart,
Walking in you'll feel her anointing from the start,
For all the hurt you feel,
She says, "By His stripes you're healed!"
That's something she will surely say,
To know God, you must fast and pray,
Within her soul the Holy Ghost dwell,
For this gift cry out as the woman at the well,
When trials come, she will instruct you,
When in despair she'll tell you how to make it through,
However, don't pretend and put on a show,
Decide to stay in your condition or grow.
She's nothing to play with,
This she'll let you know,
God's spokeswoman you can tell,
For her, it's only two options, holiness, or hell.

Feeling Alone
(Psalms 27:10) (Psalms 68:5-10)

When you're alone, know God is there,
It may seem like you're lonely and in misery,
He knows your trials please trust me!
The load is heavy and He knows how you feel,
God just wants you to come and be real.
Just begin to call His name,
He's brought you through time after time,
I trust him, He's a friend of mine.
God knowns our every trial,
Go to your prayer room,
Stay a while.

A Blessed Woman
(Proverbs 31:10-31)

Let us discuss one who's very courageous,
Categorize the word in many phrases,
Not only brave but standing strong,
She's faced hardships and yet held on,
A mother whose faced many situations,
Yet, knows how to raise a child,
It takes a whole nation,
Everywhere she goes she spreads wisdom and knowledge,
She doesn't have a PHD because she never went to college,
Her children rise and call her blessed,
Others call her a spiritual success,
Whatever they say, she's a woman who's blessed!

Your Sleep Sheep
(Isaiah 40:10-11) (Psalms 23:1-3)

Lord, thank you for another day,
Please see gratefulness as we pray,
Great shepherd grant peace to your sleep sheep,
Allow dreams pure and holy,
Touch our minds at night so sweet and boldly.
Grant the rest our bodies need.
Grant dreams of sleeping not falling,
Dreams of pressing toward high calling.
Wash our sins which are in the past.
Grant dreams of eternity, that will last.

Family and Friends
(Proverbs 18:24) (Psalms 13:31)

Without certain people, where would we be in life?
I'd rather be with them than in so much strife,
They teach integrity,
I'm speaking of friends and family.
A friend stands closer than a brother,
Know you have one another.
Jesus counted His disciples as family,
They would be together in eternity,
He knew they would be there until the end,
Lord I am thankful for family and friends.

Many Mansions
(1 John 14:1-3) (1 Thessalonians 4:1-6)

Consider my family when it comes to integrity.
We've had our share of struggles and trials,
Two said, 'Joy comes in a while',
Through heartaches they encouraged me.
The made us hold to dignity.
God has many mansions, Jesus said so.
These two have made heaven their goal.
All have roads that have to be ran,
When I said, "I couldn't",
They said, "you can."
These are battles to beat,
These two put satan to defeat.
Family, while here on this earth,
They taught our family salvation's worth.
They didn't let us give up or throw in the towel,
Motivating us to withstand every trial.
Mansions are meaningful alone.
These two will make heaven their home.
Heaven isn't crowded,
Many don't travel that road.
I'd like my mansion next to theirs,
When it's time to pull off this heavy load.

A Holy Man
(2 Peter 1:2) (2 Timothy 3:16-17)

Once stood a man of holiness and strength,
Following his pastor wherever he went,
A deacon who lived every word humbly he walked,
He didn't have to be heard,
You just had to watch his life,
I had the privilege of being his wife,
He truly lived up to his title,
A deacon's description is read in the Bible, holy.
He never preached,
He filled oppositions in church breached,
Everywhere the church went he had an effect,
His life was fulfilled and not of neglect.
I'd like to pray for God to turn back time because
I keep him in my mind,
I still hear his favorite song yet; this holy man is gone.
In our vows, we didn't know it wouldn't be long yet,
I still rejoice!
Deacon made it home.

Momma's Advice
(Titus 2:4-5) (Isaiah 66:13)

Do you remember your mother's advice?
Don't say a word if it's not nice.
The cure to a cold was lemon tea and peppermint candy,
A sowed blanket would be handy,
If you stole you went back in the store,
After she was done it wouldn't happen anymore.
Girls dressed like a lady,
Kidding was fun,
But don't get crazy; work hard and don't be lazy,
She held two jobs for us to succeed,
Those values are still instilled in me,
Thanks so much Mama for dignity.

Truly A Wreck
(Matthew 27:26) (Luke 23:33)

Before I was saved, life was a wreck,
Falling in love with Jesus I' II never regret.
You never turned away my soul nor did you reject,
Before I knew who I was, preachers were sent to me,
My life was shattered and in misery,
Surrounded with love,
You set my spirit free,
I was chosen, chased, and chastised.
You were mistreated and crucified,
I will forever be grateful for your mercy and grace,
I'll forever love the rock who pleaded my case.

Power In Your Name

Despite what scientist are saying,
It wouldn't be like this if more people were praying.
It's you Lord who created this world,
You created every man, boy, woman, and girl,
Your saints seek your presence laying on our face,
We don't feel insecure,
We know with you we're safe,
We feel your hands upon us,
As we kneel and pray,
We humbly bow, Lord have your way!
Our bodies are stretched with our lifted hands,
By your power we ask that you heal this land,
Under your shadow is where we long to be,
We seek your guidance and grace.
Going beyond our knees,
We'll fall on our face,
When your saints call on you, things won't stay the same,
Scientists don't understand there is power in your name!

Let God Build the City
(Hebrews 3:4) (Luke 14:28)

Arc you building without God's advice?
Drop your tools and think twice.
It's in vain if God doesn't build the city,
The watchman's watch will be of pity,
Before building count up the cost,
Life without Jesus is already lost,
Consider eternity, then let God build the house and city.

A New Creature
(Isaiah 43:18)

If any be in Christ, he is a new creature,
He's not his old self; he has all new features.
The old man is gone, the new man is here,
Now he's a godly man, with a godly fear,
His soul won't burn, his spirit is in the sea,
He's been adopted as God's son and a new
        life has begun.
Friends won't understand nor realize,
How did he repent? When did he decide?
What made him come to this decision?
God's thoughts are higher He has a vision,
In fact, He has the perfect plan! He
        has predestinated,
And will help heal the land.

Growing Up in God
(Proverbs 22:6) (2 Corinthians 13:11)

I remember growing up in church,
I learned to talk to God when I was hurt,
We song songs like "Standing in the promises of God."
Never did I understand that life would get so hard,
I believed the words I was singing,
When I got saved, heaven's bells were ringing.
I used to watch my mom and others,
When troubles came, they leaned on one another.
Yesterday's songs came from the heart,
Today people think they don't need to do their part.
I didn't know I would soon walk through heartache and
    storms,
Yet, I know, I was safe in God's arms.
I didn't stand brave Sometimes there was fear,
Being raised in church, is why I'm still here.
Today, I stand on God's promises and everything He's said.
I remember growing up in church, those memories
 are planted in my head.

Eternity is Forever
Years ago, young people weren't in obituaries,
Now, they're dying before getting married.
These are signs that Jesus will soon return,
Just read your bible and you will learn.
When have things ever been this way?
We didn't enter this life to stay.
God said things won't get better,
Life is short but eternity is forever.

A Girl's Knight
(The Book of Ruth)

Every girl dreams of marrying her knight regardless
    of things which transpire in life,
The moment our eyes crossed things began to be right,
We've made vows to one another never knowing one
    might lose the other,
You were a knight and your armor did shine,
I am grateful you were mine.
I'm grateful you were in my life, and I was your wife,
Through the years we stood hand in hand,
Yet, you were gone too soon,
I didn't understand.
My children looked at you as their only dad,
Your death left them really sad,
More than a King, You were my knight,
Holy you walked into the light.

God's Present Help
(Hebrews 4:16) (Psalms 46:1)

Saints hold to the throne of grace, integrity, and faith,
Ask for mercy while in need and let God guide and lead,
Take God our problems to solve,
Life changes if God's involved,
Come before Him knowing you need help,
Deliverance is in Jesus,
Not in our selves.

Standing on Judgement Day
(1 Corinthians 4:5) (2 Corinthians 5:10)

Why do they conspire and plot in vain -United,
They say there is no power in God's name,
God hears them and responds in anger -setting laws,
But they're the ones in danger,
God has made a decree,
He said, "Ask what you will of me."
Please be careful to be wise,
Which side are you on, just decide.
I'd never want to perish doing things my way.
I'd decided to stand on judgment day.

A Relationship with God
(2 Timothy 1:7) (Proverbs 35)

God is the reason I have joy in my soul,
Though overwhelmed at times, God has control.
Satan tries to block me, he's heavy on my tracks,
Yet, I belong to Jesus there's no turning back.
God guides me every day so my enemies need to
        know I know how to pray.
The blood has been pleaded in my life,
He'll shine the light.
I must be grateful for sunshine,
If I didn't have Jesus, I would have lost my mind.
I'll walk close to Jesus 'till the end of time.

An Armor Bearer's Spirit
(2 Samuel 23-27)

You can't understand because all they do and
    hear is faithful and true,
They sit and learn and know how to discern,
Always at their pastor's side working which they
    take pride,
Kneeling? They know how to pray as their leader's
    lead the way,
With spirits so humble,
When the people released Moses' hands, things crumbled.
Are they holding their leader's hands in the air, traveling
    everywhere?
No jelly backs, you must be brave,
Leader's guide the way.
Be obedient, others are watching you,
Be bold, God will guide you through.
Be quick and brave, stand guard too,
Nothing is too hard for our God!
Be there when others aren't around,
Never allow anyone to put your leader down,
Long suffering is required,
Soldiers never get tired,
Don't worry when people don't get it,
Selected and prequalified are true armor bearer's
    characteristics!

Significant Prayer
(James 5:16) (Ephesians 6:18)

I pray we saints prepare for heaven,
For the streets are gold up there,
God searches us, removing what doesn't need to be,
God gets the victory.
I pray we love our sisters and brothers,
That we wrap our arms around one another.
Murders happening for no reason at all,
Saints, don't let flesh be your downfall,
That foolishness must stop, let's get ourselves together.
I pray for saints to unite and be with Christ forever,
To fast, and fall on our knees,
To join hands and live in eternity.

Be Ready
(Matthew 24:44) (Luke 12:40)

Be ready to live a holy lifestyle,
Stop living wild,
Be ready to train children the way they should go,
To answer biblical questions people don't know,
To testify of what God has done for you,
To minister for what He has brought you through,
To go with Jesus the day He returns,
Be ready to live with Christ, not go to hell and burn.

Prayer and Fasting Time
(Acts 14:23) (Joel 12:12)

Being a soldier in God's army should stay on your mind,
Families are being attacked, it's prayer time!
Satan uses the closest person to thee,
But God has the victory!
Those in the world are really blind,
It's fasting time!
Satan attacks day by day,
We must die to ourselves every way.
Despite trials, salvation is free,
Jesus paid the price on calvary.
We're grateful not to pay a dime,
It's prayer time.
Many have faced storms and rain,
Backsliders, it's time to turn to Christ again,
With prayer and fasting life won't stay the same;
Can you understand?
It is power in Jesus' name.
No matter your problem or what's wrong,
Saints put your war clothes on!
Cover your children's soul,
Don't leave them behind.
Put your work in because it's prayer and fasting time!

Saints and Sinners Path
(Psalms 1) (Hebrews 6:10)

How can you be happy, smiling all day?
Don't follow the wicked nor mock the sinner's way,
Rejoice in His commandments and in His laws delight,
Meditate on God's Word day and night,
Know that saints are planted like trees,
They'll forever yield fruit and walk in prosperity.
The wicked won't sit in God's congregation,
Sinners will fail and reap harsh tribulations.
God is watching His saints,
We are the ones He can truly cherish!
Those that refuse to repent and turn from their ways,
   will truly perish and forfeit their grace,
They who were righteous will reach the promised land!

Not A Man (Psalms 86:15)

My lover has warm and gentle hands.
He'll never lie, He's not a man.
I've never seen his eyes, but love being by his side.
Concerned about my every care,
He shows me that he cares.
Wisely, I've learned how to dress,
He doesn't want me stressed.
Knowing him I'm really blessed.
Though life gets hard,
He's my Savior and my Lord.

Set An Example

Set an example for family and friends,
That they live a second life that will never end.
When it's time to go to work each day,
Set an example that makes others want to pray,
When the boss makes you made,
He'll know you're one of the best he's had.
When coworkers mistreat you,
Don't treat them wrong,
Set an example,
God is love for you are strong.
Others will notice God dwells in you.
God will revenge what they put you through.
When your work is over and done,
The family you're going home to,
Still have souls to be won.
When tired and in bed,
Be loving to your spouse,
They need to know God is in the house.

No Divisions
(1 Corinthians 1:10) (Ephesians 4: 1-16)

Saints, there should be no divisions among us,
In some churches people still fuss.
God doesn't want it this way,
Learn bow to pray.
We must watch for divisions,
We can't make wrong decisions,
They don't know they've been caught,
Without realizing they keep God from being sought,
It's a lot of things we should avoid,
Despite what they do,
Heaven won't be destroyed.
If saints and sinners travel,
There will be a collision.
God wants His saints united not in division.

An Idle Mind
(Ephesians 5:15-17)

Tell me why you have that expression,
What's the cause of your aggression?
Let's talk and reason together or things won't get better!
I understand what you're going through,
The enemy laughs when your down and blue.
There's nothing on tv and nothing to do,
Satan wants your mind idle to distract you.
Consider ants who work until wintertime,
Stay meditating on God,
Satan loves an idle mind.

Idle Hands
(Provers 19:15) (2 Thessalonians 3: 6-12)

God does not approve of idle hands,
Our ancestors worked hard to till the land.
Excuses are things God doesn't understand.
In life, you must work hard; Then trust in the Lord.
Pray for guidance and courage to achieve work while its day.
Laziness makes God grieve,
Continue your work if you're wise.
There's something you must know and realize,
Others are watching and God sees through His eyes.

Tables Turned
(Luke 23:33) (John 14:15-31)

He was whipped and crucified,
His enemies all lied.
Barnabas, a sinner was set free,
Then He died on cavalry.
They soon reached a place called skull,
Jesus could have made Pilot's decision null.
God never intended for man to burn,
We were God's while being sinners,
We just had to learn.
Ascending, Jesus gave the Holy Ghost and the tables turned.

Hear My Cry
(Psalms 5:1-5) (Psalms 25: 4-5)

Lord, please listen as I speak these words,
Let my heart's cry be heard.
I plead for you to hear my cry,
Surrounded by enemies, they want me to die.
At sunrise, please hear my voice,
Others serve idols, yet I made you my choice.
Evil men can never stand in the presence of you,
You hearing my cry pulls me through.

Be Born Again
(John 3: 7-16)

Whatever you do, you must be born again.
Search the world over,
Become a military man.
Winds blow strong,
Hear the sound,
In vain does the Earth spin around.
Those in the Spirit are one in the same.
Be born again and call on His name.
Seek heaven where you want to be,
Walk in the Spirit,
Seek eternity.

What Do We See?
(Song of Solomon 1:15)

Do we see love through each other's eyes?
I see my Boaz,
Then I realize you pick me up when I'm down,
The love you have for me has always been around.
While others sleep, you hold me through the night.
With you problems seem small and everything is right.
You're the perfect man for me!
Once I doubted love,
Now I Believe!
Through God a fairy tale is now reality.
Our vows have been recited 'til death do us part,
The vows we took came straight from the heart.

Gifted
(Matthew 25:14-30)

Having gifts placed inside of us without a fuss
    truly makes us blessed and prepares us for success.
Work with what God gave you,
Stay in your own lane,
Know you have a gift,
Call on God's name.
Some gifts prepare you for eternity,
I can't work your gift,
Only what God gave me.

Homegoing Celebration
(1 Thessalonians 4: 13-17)

Heaven is rejoicing today, you made it home!
No more suffering, all your pain is gone.
It hurt watching you in agony for so long,
We can't ask, "How can it be?"
    because this we saw beforehand.
God spoke, "Be prepared," to your family.
You won the battle you had to fight,
Now ascend to live your second life,
It's a blessing to proceed to heaven,
Greet you parents, siblings, and wife,
As l held your hand you finished your course,
Take a bow soldier, Jesus was your choice.
We can still hear you sing, "Just another day..."
Now you're an angel that helped show me the way.
No, there won't be sadness and frustration.
You were a true born soldier,
This is a home going celebration.

I Fled My Enemies
(Psalms 33)

Increased are those who troubled me,
Those considered friends turned to enemies,
Saying, "There's no help in God.",
Little do they know; I hold tight when things are hard.
You are my buckler and shield,
All I ask is people be still.
You're my glory and help lift my head,
I don't have to fight, God will instead.
I cried and asked that you have your will,
You heard me from your holy hill.
Sleep, there was sleep at night,
I awoke held by your might.
Of my enemies, I dare not be afraid,
You'll rescue me and come to my aid.
Through enemies falling, I was humble and meek,
My avengers you struck them on their cheeks.

Learn How to Sleep
(Psalms 4) (Isaiah 26:3-4)

I don't fear, Jesus is always there,
Though the world is against me I'm in your care,
You hold me up and never let me fall,
In distress, you hear when I call.
Evil men try to turn your glory to shame,
They don't believe there's power in your name,
All they seek is false,
Yet without you this world would be lost.
There's a separation the holy are set apart,
No matter the works, God searches the heart.
Holy men keep meditating,
Let your hearts be still.
God will fulfill His will.
Though roads will be rocky and hard,
Keep your trust in the Lord.
Though grain and wine will cease,
Stop tossing and turning, then learn how to sleep.

Forever Love
(Song of Solomon 8:6-7) (2 Corinthians 6: 14-17)

I said a prayer as a girl,
About my husband, whom I'd share my world,
I was specific, not timid, or afraid,
I prayed about the vows we made,
I prayed for certain qualities,
His love had to be for God and me,
I wanted him noble and to possess dignity.
His appearance tall and strong,
I wanted him to embrace me in his arms,
He had to have a pure heart and gentle soul.
I prayed we'd grow old together,
I didn't want the fire to cease,
Come rain or stormy weather,
When one passed, our love spoke of forever.

The Reason You're Free
(Exodus 21:1-6) (Leviticus 25: 44-46)

I saw what you experienced and helped you run,
Your beatings weren't any fun,
At that time, it was against the law,
I had to help, given what I saw.
Blacks were taken advantage of,
Some lynched,
I saw you jump the fence.
Many lives were lost,
You had to count the cost.
You don't know why you were treated that way,
Understand times when you learn to pray,
Those who mistreated you, forgot about judgement day.
Those freed didn't want to stay.
These were the days of Civil Rights,
Blacks couldn't give in they had to fight.
Then, came one who was sent, the first black president.
Many black leaders today are gone,
They knew a change would come.
How could I be there through what seems like eternity,
My name is God-
I'm the reason you're free.

My Father's Absence
(John 1:6-12)

His memories are ignored,
My children are adored,
His love was never gave,
Compliments never made,
His voice I'd love to hear,
His picture held near,
His absence brought tears.
You looked forward to seeing him one day,
He went away,
Children are as arrows to a mighty man,
Yet, I had uncles take me by the hand,
God will be a Father to the fatherless,
My heavenly Father is why I'm blessed.

How I Made It
(Hebrew 4:12) (2 Samuel 1:12)

I was once strong in Christ,
Trials made me weak.
As saints, God wants us meek,
I needed God's guidance to stay a sheep.
Trials cause you to struggle,
Day by day I've now been a soldier day by day,
I know He'll make a way.
Watching, fasting, and staying in prayer,
One day we'll meet Jesus in the air.

Judgement Day
(Revelation 2:1-4) (1 John 3:2)

Saints,

It's a wonderful day being on God's side,

For our sins, He quietly died,

We must look forward to judgment day,

All tears will be wiped away,

Death itself will be no more,

There'll be no reason to mourn.

Trumpets will alarm,

Satan can never again do any harm.

What will be doesn't appear,

God will say well done my child,

Come sit up here.

Prayer Warrior
(Acts I:14) (Matthew 21:22)

In this life there are trials you've been through,

I sit here to minister to you,

I don't mean to preach,

Just want you to know at I've told you of God's mercy
    and grace.

The unbelievers are saved by a believing spouse,

Depression can't overtake you,

When a prayer warrior is in the house.

I've asked God to please step in,

Put your mind at ease,

I'll cover you by being on my knees.

My Temple
(Psalms 23:5) (Acts 2:4)

My body is a temple,
I'm saved from what I used to do,
My former sins were against you.
Depression once weighed me down,
Friends weren't found,
Jesus lifted me; I was so ashamed,
I found deliverance by calling on Jesus' name.
Warned of destruction as in Noah's flood,
Now I'm saved and covered in the blood!
Sinners let me introduce you to the God of host,
I'm no longer in sin,
He's filled me with the Holy Ghost.

Praise God on High
(Psalms 7) (Psalms 150)

Lord again I'm trusting thee,
Asking you to deliver me,
Waiting to destruct my soul are enemies,
In my heart, I request you to arise,
Let enemies realize,
Allow evil men to end,
Prove you're the saint's friend,
Sinners brought falsehood,
It didn't do any good,
So, I'll praise God on high!
God always hears the saint's cry.

Forgiven
(Luke 23:26-43) (Matthew 27: 32-56)

I'm big and beautiful,
I've never been small,
You said you loved it all,
You loved me every day and casted
    out ungodly ways,
I see through brown eyes,
Yet you stretched and died,
Others loved me yet soon were gone,
Because of you, I'm never alone.
I never knew what you saw in me,
You knew what you saw on calvary.
Like the thief of the cross,
I was guilty of sin,
Your precious love is why I'm forgiven.

Rich and Poor
(Luke 16: 19-31) (Proverbs 18:23)

The poor in life could be prey,
The rich account grows, the poor decay.
Poor man hold to better days, this is mentioned in songs,
A lot have sung, change will come,
But be strong with faith in God can't be wrong,
They both have something in the same,
It's the decision to call on Jesus's name.
We can hold to integrity and pride,
The road their souls travel,
Both have to decide.

Souls Wanted
(2 Timothy 2: 3-13) (Joshua 8:10-19)

Looking at the saints,
You ask what we want,
For your soul to burn, is what we don't want,
It's souls we have to win,
It's our duty if we're God's friend.
We're saints and wear His description,
Always win souls until we fill all positions.
Some want your body,
God wants your soul,
One thing on our mind, our ultimate goal,
Soldiers look for those they can save,
Holy soldiers, we stand strong and brave!

Materials Don't Last
(Jeremiah 22:13) (Hebrews 13:5)

Building?
You must count the cost; without God we're lost.
Build being holy and stay on God's side,
Know God will provide, always strive.
Never build by doing wrong, God sees all along.
Never rob others of wages,
Life comes in stages,
Never lower your standards for cash,
Only what we do for God will last.

Offering Time
(Matthew 6:21) (Numbers 18:21)

Saints today refuse paying one tenth,
Taking all your money was never meant,
Are tithes too much for you?
There's something God doesn't do.
We have jobs to pay bills,
Getting all our money is not His will,
When you give you reap in return,
When will you learn?
Join other tithers and be united,
Next time its offering time get excited!
Though not tithing isn't a crime,
I give God praises to give at offering time.

No Time for Stress
(Romans 3:23)

Others examined her life,
Childless, and she was no one's wife,
They watched and knew work was done,
She was called to salvation while out having fun,
Yet, God heard her cry and plea,
Substances covered misery,
Alone at home she turned the key,
Now she stood in integrity.
She knew she was saved and truly blessed,
Her mind stayed on Jesus,
There was no time to be stressed.

The Adulterous Woman's Debt

What you sow you'll surely reap.
Numbered as saints and counted as sheep.
Can all your sins be waived?
Things happened while you were saved,
How many times have you strayed?
How can you look at others and think of threat?
The adulterous woman's accuser's found regret.
Yet, she knew with Jesus she'd always be in debt.

I've Learned to be Content
(Hebrews 13:5) (Philippians 4:11-13)

Once I was blind and couldn't see,
My soul could've burnt in eternity.
God reached down to save me,
He set me free!
I've seen hardships but learned to be content,
All I've faced in life,
In hell's fire,
My second life won't be spent.

Your House and God's
(Haggai 1:9)

We can't spend money in vain, giving may cause pain.
We must work and share, concerning giving- God cares.
There's no harm having bank accounts,
Your career can vary the amount.
Don't forget God,
Sow your seeds,
There'll always be needs.
Concerning your house,
You can't be constructive,
Then, when you look at God's house it's in destruction.

Foot Stool
(Proverbs 13:11) (Proverbs 22:16)

There was a woman without good health,
Though blessed, she didn't have much wealth,
She never spent all her money,
Others found it funny,
She learned to stretch her cash,
Others couldn't make it last,
How, when they had more?
Some spent money on whores,
They started asking her for loans,
All their money was gone,
Their money was spent as fools,
All her enemies were now her foot stools.

Celebrities
(Mark 10:25) (Matthew 19:23)

Here lies a powerful voice,
They choose to sing never making God a choice,
I use to admire celebrities,
Now, I admire those on their knees.
How celebrities die disturbs my very soul.
God's my choice and heaven's my goal,
They overdose without peace or rest,
Others should've told them life was a test,
It's harder for a rich man to enter heaven,
Than a camel can through a needle's eye,
Prayers are needed before another on dies.

Wise In Their Own Eyes
(Psalms 15:22) (Proverbs 12:15)

How much do we waste?
Others want to be in our place.
Weekly, we trash unwanted food,
Others count it as good.
Our mothers would turn in their graves,
Some things can cause us to succeed,
We could help others in need,
This may sound foolish to you,
    but do you know what fools do?
The Bible calls them wise in their own eyes,
When you take advice, pride is put to the side.

When You Needed Me
(1 Chronicles 16:8) (Psalms 105:1)

You don't realize it,
I've always been there for you,
In the hospital, my hand pulled you through,
I wanted you to prosper and be in good health,
I worked though the doctor's hands myself.
No, it was me,
No one else will take credit,
When I move for you, be willing to tell it!
I was both judge and the lawyer in the courtroom,
Your business didn't go under,
I allowed it to bleed.
I stood at the altar when you said I do,
You were given strength when others walked away from you.
I held you in my arms through trials and tribulations,
I allowed you to flee when faced with temptation.
I've been there for the world since creation,
Please communicate,
What's on your mind, please no hesitation.
I heard your cry the very first time!
Pick up the phone, call thy name,
When you begin to call on me,
Your circumstances change.

He Loved Me That Much
(Matthew 27:26) (John 19:30)

God had to reach down to save my soul,
I have unspoken testimonies I've never told,
I can't tell how much He's done for me,
I am one who has to stay on her knees.
The life I was living I almost burst hell wide open!
With all my family's prayers they would've cried.
As the adulterous woman I was caught in the act,
Fingers were pointed at me, that's a fact!
Jesus said, "Cast the first stone?"
I saw all my accusers were gone,
God reached down to save me from my mess,
He had to deliver me; I was a terrible wretch.
My life was truly changed and touched.
I asked how much He loved me,
He died on Calvary saying that much.

Loved Me from the Sky
(Acts 2:17) (Joel 2:28)

Last night I had such a magical dream!
I didn't have to question what did it mean,
You were on one knee,
You asked, "Will you marry me?"
The rock on my finger,
Most beautiful of rings,
Your mouth opened and song these magic words!
You were a King of Kings,
I was truly blessed,
Soon I awoke realizing your soul was at rest.
I never questioned why,
Vows were made until the day we die,
Yet, our love was so strong!
You loved me from the sky.

Keep Abiding
(John 15:5) (I John 2:28)

How can one have a righteous mind?
You must stay connected to the vine,
You don't need tools or ranches,
God is the vine, and we arc the branches.
There's no better way of being touched,
Our fruit reveals so much.
Though the resurrection could take years,
Keep abiding until He reappears,
If you consider Jesus as a friend,
Continue being holy and free of sin.
Life itself can be extremely hard,
Yet, for eternity keeping abiding in the Lord.

Built on the Rock
(Matthew 7:24-27) (Joshua 24:15)

Once a man built his house on a rock,
Enduring to the end he never stopped.
Then a man built his house on sand,
Refusing holiness, he never took God's hands.
Soon ruin turned to flood,
The house on the rock was covered in Jesus's blood,
The one on sand was blew and beat.
Godless, the house laid in defeat!
If you obey God's command,
Your house will stand.

You Ran Well
(Galatians 5:7) (Hebrews 12:1)

Once your heart was full of praise,
Now you walk in ungodly ways,
You said He met your needs,
Now, He's ashamed indeed!
When it's time for church,
You're in the bed,
You don't want to attend and make excuses instead.
Your life can be examined through and through,
No one believes a word coming from you!
Influenced by the wrong crowd,
All can tell,
What happened to you Zion,
You once ran so well!

God's Will
(1 Peter 2:15)

We as saints must be the light and do right,
No longer conformed,
Our minds must be transformed.
Then we'll stand the test,
Knowing God, we're blessed.
God's will is pleasing,
Never let our looks be deceiving.
Then, the storm can be still,
This is God's will.

Faithful Over Few
(Ezekiel 44:23) (Luke 16:10)

Once I sat in my house,
God can speak when things are as quiet as a mouse.
Being close to God means being clean,
We have to care for everything.
We're blessed to share an apartment or chair,
It's a privilege,
Others want to be there,
Though at times cleaning seems hard,
Just begin and start.
Care for what you've been entrusted with,
Never forget!
Give your gift a special touch,
Being faithful over a few mean blessings with much.

He Showed Me Myself
(1 Corinthians 15:31) (2 Corinthians 12:8)

I had to ask God to remove thorns from me,
As Paul, I desired to die daily.
I wanted my heart clean,
I hid under His wings,
Faced with test,
Remove all thorns,
Paul said it best!
I was comforted with the same test day by day,
Until you pass, you'll face them.
They'll come your way.
I wasn't doing good at all,
Those little sins seem so small,
Someone witnessed my nasty flesh,
It was trash,
It wasn't for others, I needed help!
Fingers could be pointed, but He showed me myself.

Streets Painted with Gold
(John 5:24) (John 11:25)

Let's prepare, we have to go,
We can rest our souls,
I'd like to see others we know,
Those who died long ago.
It's a glorious place where trials are eroded,
Streets are gold and angels praise His name!
With those mansions life is forever changed.
There'll always be sun, it'll never rain.
There's one way to tell you,
Rest from going through,
Saints we have purpose,
No one's ever worthless.
We're trying to reach our goal,
Where streets are painted gold,
Glory to God in Heaven!
We'll be made whole.

God Work on Me
(1 Peter 1:16) (Hebrews 4:12)

Life in Christ shouldn't be fake,
God is truly awake,
Stay connected and be real,
Ask God to take the wheel,
People will say, "God knows my heart."
In heaven, sinners won't take part.
Wakeup!
Have sense!
You can't straddle the fence.
Sins are in the book of revelation.
We owe an obligation.
God knows whose playing,
Watch, fast, and keep praying.
Jesus went to hell and took the keys,
Heaven's the place to be!
For those...Say, "God work on me!"

Day of Pentecost
(Jeremiah 3:2) (Hebrews 6:4-6)

Some holy men,
Set one day on one accord,
The Spirit was high,
They were praising the Lord.
Amazed,
Some were confused,
Maybe jealous they weren't being used.
Whispering, they looked and stared,
"Drunk",
Are words they shared.
Then came the sound of a rushing wind,
They weren't drunk,
These were chosen men.
Some may have sung a song,
Why were they speaking in tongues?
Appearing as cloves of fire,
Their spirits were taken higher.
On God alone did they boast?
It was the Holy Ghost!
Those saints would not be lost,
This was the powerful day called, Pentecost.

With My Whole Heart
(Psalms 9) (John 4:24)

Holy, Holy!
I'll forever praise you Lord!
Situations in life will be difficult and hard,
Yet, I'll always testify of what you've done for me,
How you loosed and set me free!
Enemies will fall yet, I stand tall,
Through years and generations,
You're destroying wicked nations,
Daily they perish,
However, your saints are cherished.
God will endure those that are pure,
He's a refuge to the oppressed,
They are blessed.
I must still do my part,
Praise you with my heart!

Asking For a Gift
(Acts 2:4) (Mark 16:17)

Lately I've asked for a gift that's for a shift,
Delight in Him and He'll grant your heart's desire,
Know He's going to take you higher.
Learn how to call His name,
Holiness is never in vain,
Seek Him first and all will be added,
Due to grace and mercy, you can't be saddened,
Seek and He knows what you need most,
Be grateful for the Holy Ghost,
It will come with many signs,
On you, God's glory will shine.
Praise Him from your lungs,
Ask God for the gift of speaking in tongues.

God Knows His Name

From dust, God formed Adam himself,
Seeing you for me, there's no one else,
Lonely, God had to form Eve,
We'd unite again, is what you believed.
Naked they walked the ground,
Love came around,
United.
Adam and Eve were the same.
As Adam and Eve,
He's my Adam and God knows his name.

The Back Slider
(Jeremiah 3:2) (Hebrews 6:4-6)

God is one of second chances,
He shifts circumstances.
While preaching this saint once cried,
Through the congregation he saw tears in her eyes,
He knew God saw every heart,
He doesn't deal with us as our sins deserve,
Her mind was decided when they opened the church,
She understood while she was there,
Realizing she needed prayer.
He prophesied as she wept and stood,
He preached a n d told her all he could,
Ask how I know her sins were cast in the sea,
I know because the lady was me.

My Boaz
(Ruth 2:3) (Ruth 3:13)

Handsome, yet not tall a friend I can call.
Faithful, for another there's no need,
There are many beautiful women, he's not deceived.
I love his baby hair, others surely stare.
They'd love to be on his arms,
My Boaz's inner strength is extremely strong,
I know I'm blessed God gave him to me,
As Ruth in the Bible, I'll lay at his feet.
Do we see love through each other's eyes?
I see my Boaz,
Then I realize you pick me up when I'm down.
The love you have for me has always been around.
While others sleep, you hold me through the night.
With you, problems seem small; everything is right.
You're the perfect man for me!
Once I doubted love, now I believe!
Through God a fairy tale is now reality.
Our vows have been recited till death do us part,
The vows we took came straight from the heart.

What Does It Prosper?
(Ecclesiastes 2:11, 4:4, 5:10, 6:2) (Jeremiah 2:5)

Envying each other?
Not building up one another?
Surveying work you've done.
Working without fun?
This is meaningless under the sun.
What does it prosper?
To be educated and being called wise?
Yet, heaven or hell you can't decide!
Loving money, but not having enough,
Facing trials not knowing life gets rough?
God grants possessions and wealth,
Serving idols until you're worthless yourself,
Fornicating- feeling in vain,
Those lovers and sins cause pain.
What does it prosper being angry and bold?
To gain this world and lose your soul.

A Lifetime

Excuse me,
Don't mean to stare,
God won't overload you with what you can't bear,
Know this prayer,
Know about His mercy and grace,
Trouble don't last,
There won't be a trace,
Bare this one thing in mind,
Favor lasts a lifetime.

Going To Make a Difference
(James 5:26) (Galatians 6:1)(Matthew 40:11)

I'm determined to make a change in my lifetime,
I'm one person, but there'll be one less crime,
Maybe I'll give a smile,
Someone in grief knows joy comes in a while,
Maybe I can buy a homeless person a meal one day,
I want to make a change in my own way,
Providing shelter one night,
Turning wrong to right.
I'm an instrument,
I know I was sent,
Looking in the mirror at my own face,
We must voluntarily help our race,
At death what will the word's read,
Did I ignore someone's need?
This must be done with all my power and might,
I'll feel better when it's my time to say good night.

What's the Advantage?
(Micah 6:8) (Colossians 1:10-11)

Why decide on Christ?
To live a second life?
Why decide to walk holy?
To testify boldly,
Why understand to withstand trials in this lifetime?
God is renewing hearts and minds.
What's the advantage of being on the battlefield?
We have the advantage to of letting God take the wheel.
Why race until we finish the course?
The world can see Jesus is our choice!
Soldiers must count the cost though the
    world is turned and tossed,
Being soldiers we are on assignment,
The advantage of all this is spiritual success!

God Can Not Fail
(Psalms 33:4)

Despite problems and Satan on your trail,
God cannot fail,
God is in control so stand faithful and bold,
He'll make an escape for all you go through,
He both knows and sees you.
Trials come day by day but know all is well,
God can do anything and he'll never fail!

Matters of a Woman's Heart
(Psalms 91) (Ephesians 6:13)

Please explain the matters of a woman's heart,
What keeps her together?
What pulls her apart?
All have things treasured,
Things that bring us pleasure,
How do you have peace in a storm?
A true woman of God hides in God's arms.
Is it the one who brought her in the world,
Who held her from when she was a little girl,
She'll walk in Mama's steps one day,
It matters that she taught her to pray,
Mom is viewed as a work of art,
These are some issues of the heart.
Could it be the man who was her first,
Her Boaz that humbles her,
When it comes to him, her heart just bursts!

Blessed
(Psalms 1)

Blessed is the one who's not in sinners steps,
Lift up you head from which comes your help,
Blessed is the man who refuses sinners way,
He meditates on God night and day,
Blessed is the man planted by the water's stream,
They hold to Jesus and know He's King.
Sinners will come to a sudden end,
They'll never live to live again.
The righteous will pass the ultimate test,
They are eternally blessed.

Saints in Heaven
(Genesis 7-22:13) (Genesis 32:25-33) (Genesis 28:1-11)

I fell asleep last night a quarter 'til 11,
I had a beautiful dream about saints in heaven,
Abraham had a ram in the bush,
Jacob was wrestling an angel and gave a real big push,
Moses led Israel out of Egypt land,
David had a spear in hand,
Joseph dreamed of a coat, and
Noah built his boat.
It was a beautiful place,
I saw momrna's face,
She told me it wasn't my time,
She was sweet and kind.
When I awoke things weren't as it seemed,
O' The saints in heaven such a beautiful dream!

Angels Among Us
(Hebrews 13:2) (Hebrews 1:14)

There are certain angels among you,
Know that it's true!
You entertain angels unaware,
Think they've always been there?
Maybe you haven't heard,
These are Pastors equipped with God's Word,
Continually praying over our souls,
Heaven is their goal!
They are there through storms we go through,
And there when we don't know what to do.
There when we need healing when others aren't willing.
Honor? They deserve double,
There around when our children are in trouble.
God grants Pastors according to His own heart,
They were meant to be Pastors from the start.
Don't buck or try to fuss,
Be grateful for angels being among us.

Fighting Time
(2 Corinthians 10:4-5)

There is a gladness in my spirit,
True spiritual soldiers may get it,
Satan turns up the heat day by day,
Yet, we know to trust and pray.
Saints are being attacked but don't turn back!
Jesus came and God's will was done, the battle is won.
If they question what's wrong with the saints,
We're sanctified, heaven is on our mind,
Like never before, It's fighting time!

Walk In the Light
(Ephesians 5: 8-14)

Once in darkness our hearts were impure,
Jesus took our sins so we could endure.
He died on the cross so our souls wouldn't be lost,
He had to show us light,
He showed us we could live right.
Consist in holiness and truth,
Glorify Him,
Glorify His name,
Don't walk in guilt or in shame.
Meditate day and night Saints,
It's time to walk in the light.

I Entered As Me
(1 Thessalonians 4:14)

As I leave, take these words from me:
I entered this world a sinful me,
While here, I gained Christ and eternity.
I was changed,
Now, I can live a second life.
These words are for family, friends, and my wife.
Remember we walked in Christ together,
Treasure these memories forever,
Think of how we held to God's powerful hand,
When tears flow and you don't understand.
Let Jesus lead you all the way,
Falling asleep is something some must do,
When you fall asleep, beloved I'll wait on you.

Praying for a Humble Heart
(Isaiah 58:6) (Psalm 9:12)

Lord, give me humbleness and a spirit contrite,
Let me be holy and mend broken pieces in my life,
The contrite hearts, you will revive!
I pray to be holy and sanctified,
You won't fail me, you'll avenge our enemies,
Humble hearts, you will always remember,
I pray my heart will always be tender.

I Am
(Exodus 20:2) (Luke 24:44)

During trials please don't be alarmed,
Those covered in the blood will be left unharmed.
The Bible will fulfill its purpose itself,
Don't worry, God is our present help.
So much will take place before your eyes,
Yet, we have Jesus on our side.
Scriptures must be fulfilled Genesis to Revelation,
God is coming back without hesitation,
Every knee must bow and every tongue must confess,
You can run but not hide,
God's messengers warned you to decide.
All this will happen,
Yes ma'am.
God alone is the great I Am.

My Prayer

As you read this book let it inspire you
I pray my words will pull you through,
Please see God and not me,
Let no flesh receive glory,
I pray you'll find strength to tell your story,
I pray all saints will know their talent,
We have gifts but are only instruments,
I pray when we expire from this flesh.
And that we be seated as God's guest!

We Fight
(2 Corinthians 10: 4-5)

Fight or flight as saints we stand,
How do we fight?
We keep our eyes on God,
Though fiery trials are extremely hard,
You fight by knowing your God,
Knowing He'll see us through,
The God who brought us out yesterday,
Will do the same today too!
We fight by pushing our plates to the side,
We hold His hand, knowing He'll guide.
We seek God day and night,
This is how we fight.

Weeper's Laugh
(Luke 6:21)

Just as prayer, laughing is good for the soul,
When you make a sad man cry,
His heart can be made whole,
A crowd sat around, all so bad,
They heard music, realizing things weren't so bad.
If you're hungry, your belly God will fill,
For those who mourn, your joy will be real,
For those who laugh, know you did weep,
God gave you a smile and peace so sweet.

Which Side Will You Be On?
(Joshua 24:15) (Matthew 13:44)

When Jesus comes, which side will you be on?
All chances will be gone,
There will be great division, what's your decision?
Will you be on God's side? There'll be no need to hide.
No matter what you've been through,
No excuses for you.
No need to say, "Didn't I prophesy?"
You stood flat footed and told a lie!
You say of "Living holy I am bored."
I've made my decision to serve the Lord!

Sing Praises
(Psalms 33)

With my whole heart Lord, 'll praise thee.
You're worth more than gold to me.
Your marvelous works will forever show!
I'll represent you wherever I go.
Many tongues aren't enough to praise you above the sky.
I'll always cry out to The Most High,
My enemies will turn back and fall,
I hear your voice when you call.
Your judgement is true and ever so right.
You grant me peace through the night.
Evil men no longer exist,
Your saints you'll forever carry and be with.

Made in the USA
Columbia, SC
28 October 2024

44871575R00039

43415795R00117